The Ultimate Motorcycles

MINIBIKES

Lori Kinstad Pupeza

ABDO Publishing Company

visit us at
www.abdopub.com

Published by Abdo Publishing Company 4940 Viking Drive, Edina, Minnesota 55435.
Copyright © 1998 by Abdo Consulting Group, Inc. International copyrights reserved in all
countries. No part of this book may be reproduced in any form without written permission
from the publisher.

Printed in the United States.

Photo credits: Patrick Laurel, Duomo, Yamaha, Nick Dygert

Edited by Kal Gronvall

Library of Congress Cataloging-in-Publication Data

Pupeza, Lori Kinstad
   Minibikes / Lori Kinstad Pupeza.
      p. cm. -- (The ultimate motorcycle series)
  Includes index.
  Summary: Explains the difference between minibikes and minicycles, parts of the bike
and how they work, and how to choose the right one, as well as describing riding gear
and rules on where to ride.
  ISBN 1-57765-002-6
  1. Minibikes--Juvenile literature.   [1.Minibikes. 2. Motorcycles] I. Title. II. Series:
Pupeza, Lori Kinstad. Ultimate motorcycle series
  TL443.P87 1998
  629.227'5--dc21

              98-10606
                CIP
                 AC

Warning: The series *The Ultimate Motorcycles* is intended as entertainment for children. These activities should never be attempted without training, instruction, supervision, and proper equipment.

Contents

Minibikes and Minicycles

Minibike riding is a great way for kids to have fun. Minibikes and minicycles are small motorcycles. They are made for driving on dirt trails. Very few are made for driving on streets or sidewalks.

Racing a minibike can also be a lot of fun. Official racing organizations set up rules and competitions in different classes. On the other hand, just racing with your friends with your own rules can be just as much fun. Anybody can ride a minibike. It doesn't matter how old you are. Kids as young as four years old compete and ride with skill.

The difference between a minibike and a minicycle is the size of the whole bike. Other factors distinguishing the two are the size of the wheels, and the size of the engine. Minibikes don't usually have wheels that are any bigger than 12 inches (30.5 cm). Minicycles have tires that can be as big as 16 inches (40.6 cm) and have better suspension systems than minibikes.

Minibikes aren't made to be driven on the road, and only a few minicycle models are legal to be driven on the road. Some minicycles have head lights and tail lights, and turn signals. Most do not since they aren't made for street driving.

There is a blurry line between a minibike and minicycle. There are many different styles, designs, and engine sizes. Every year manufacturers come out with better built, more durable minibikes and minicycles. Finding out what will work best for you is just part of the fun.

These Yamaha YSR's are the 50 cc version of their big brother the Yamaha FZR. From the handlebars to the ground, the YSR sits under three feet (1m) tall.

History of the Minibike

When minibikes first came out adults played with them more than children did. In the mid-1960s, Honda imported a minibike that folded up for easy transport. Honda called it the Monkey Bike. They were first sold in Australia.

People all over the world, however, had been building miniature motorcycles on their own for years. The Monkey Bike cost more money than most people wanted to spend, and it was marketed mainly for adults.

It wasn't long before other minibike manufacturers built their own versions. An early minibike maker named John Deck and Sons improved the frame design and performance of the bike. Future builders kept improving the minibike. By the 1970s, people were buying minibikes not only for themselves, but also for their children.

The 1970s was the golden age for minibikes. Lots of kids had them, and most wanted them. Minicycles were built later. They were made to look and act like full-size dirt bikes. Today, minicycles and minibikes have suspension systems and are more durable than early models. Many early models have become collectibles. The Honda Minitrail 50, the Honda Trail 70, and several models that Rupp made are quite popular today.

The 1970s were considered the golden age of minibikes.

Picking the Right Machine

What do you want to do with your minibike? Do you want to ride on trails with your friends? Do you want to race? Maybe both? A minibike is great for younger kids who want to kick up dirt on the back trails. Minibikes aren't raced as much as minicycles. Minicycles look like mini dirt bikes and are the main kind of cycle driven in races. If you're sure that you want to race, a minicycle is for you.

Once you figure out what you're going to use it for, the next step is to look for a minibike. Going to a minibike dealer is a good idea. Sit on different minibikes and make sure your feet can reach the ground flat footed. Your parents may want to buy a minibike that is bigger than you need so that you can "grow into it." That is a bad idea. A minibike is not like a pair of shoes. For safety reasons, find a minibike that isn't too tall or too heavy.

Another thing to consider when looking at minibikes is whether or not you want an automatic or manual clutch. For beginning riders, an automatic will be easier to drive. Sometimes you won't always have a choice. If you find a bike that fits right and it happens to have a manual clutch, don't shy away from it. Anyone can learn to use a manual clutch.

A minibike must also be comfortable. Today, most minibikes have suspension systems. Early minibikes had no suspension systems, aside from a few springs under the seat. This made for a bumpy ride! It didn't take long for minibike manufacturers to get the hint and put suspension on the bikes.

Minibike makers soon added front suspension. The front forks were built out of telescopic tubing. The lower forks were made to slide in and out of the upper fork, and the same technology is used today.

The rear wheel on a minibike or minicycle has a big coil spring connected to the frame. If you're buying a used machine, make sure the suspension system isn't damaged or worn out completely. Most new minibikes or minicycles cost around $1,000.

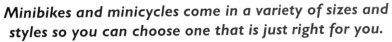

Minibikes and minicycles come in a variety of sizes and styles so you can choose one that is just right for you.

Engine Size and Speed

Not only do you need to pay attention to the physical size of the bike, but also to the engine size. Buying a very fast bike could end up being too much for your level of riding skills.

A good beginning size is the 50 cc engine. Cubic centimeters (cc's) is a term that refers to the volume of a motorcycle's cylinder when the piston is as far down as it can go. The bigger the space, or the greater the cubic centimeters, the more gas that can fill up the space. And the more fuel that fills up the cylinder, the more power it can produce.

A 50 cc engine can go about 30-40 miles per hour (48-64 kph). A 100-125 cc size bike can go about 55-60 miles per hour (88-96 kph). Minicycles usually have engines that are scaled down motorcycle engines.

These bikes have 50 cc engines.

Minibikes built with industrial engines are classified by horsepower. A one, two, or three horsepower engine is a good size to start with. Buying a bike that is too big for you will make riding tough and dangerous. Riding won't be much fun if you don't pick the right bike. Take the time to find just the right bike for you.

This Yamaha YZ80 is a good moderate size bike for the beginning rider.

Riding Gear

Riding on a bumpy trail at a fast pace often times ends up in mishaps and bike crunchers. It is part of riding a bike. Some even consider it part of the fun of minibike riding. You could hit a rock and fly off the bike sideways, or run into a ditch and flip over the bars, or hit your head on a tree trunk. Anything could happen.

Minor scrapes and scratches hurt, but heal quickly. Broken bones take a little longer. Broken heads, however, usually don't heal. That's why a crash helmet is so important. A good helmet will prevent most serious head injuries and is the most important piece of safety gear.

A helmet should cover your whole head. It should also protect your face and chin. Good helmets have nose guards that reach across your face and snap to the helmet to keep you from breaking your nose if you fall face first. A clear shield will also keep dust and sand from getting in your eyes. The inside lining of a helmet is very hard. It's made to absorb all the impact of a crash, so you're head doesn't.

It is very important to have a jacket and pants made out of thick material. Leather is good, but it is also very hot and expensive. Denim works well. It isn't as durable as leather,

but by adding a few patches at the knees and elbows, you can avoid road rash. Jackets made out of high-tech, lightweight fabric are better than denim, but cost more.

You also need boots and gloves for riding the trails. Most minibike riders need a solid pair of boots. A rider needs to put his or her foot down sometimes to steady the bike, or to turn tight corners. Some riders prefer a boot with no heel. Boots with heels can get caught on rocks and other objects on the trail. Therefore, flat boots usually work the best.

Leather gloves without a lining are the best kind of gloves for kids on minibikes. The first thing that hits the ground when you're falling off a minibike is your hands. You'll want something in between your skin and the ground if that happens. The right gear is important.

This rider is wearing protective gear.

The Parts of a Minibike

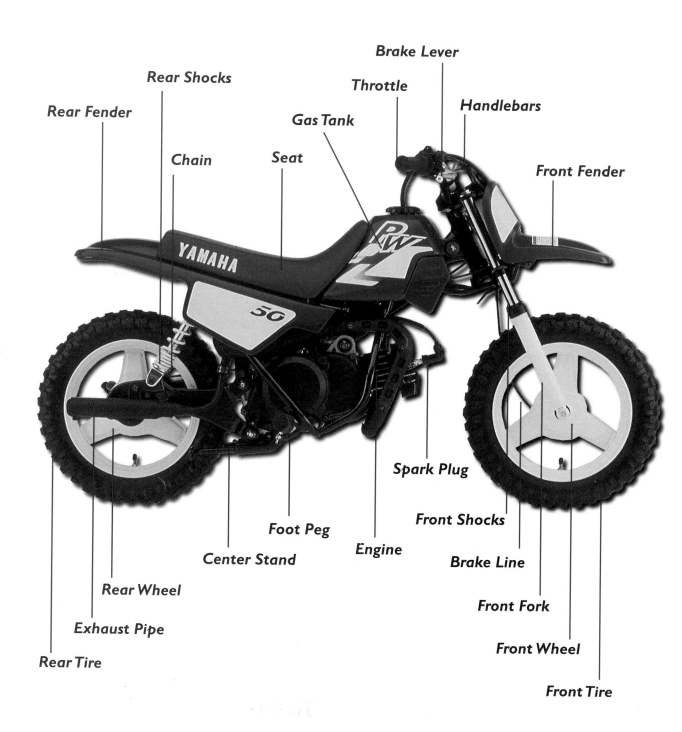

Brake Lever

Throttle

Handlebars

Rear Shocks

Gas Tank

Rear Fender

Front Fender

Chain

Seat

Spark Plug

Front Shocks

Foot Peg

Engine

Brake Line

Center Stand

Rear Wheel

Front Fork

Exhaust Pipe

Front Wheel

Rear Tire

Front Tire

How a Two-Stroke Engine Works

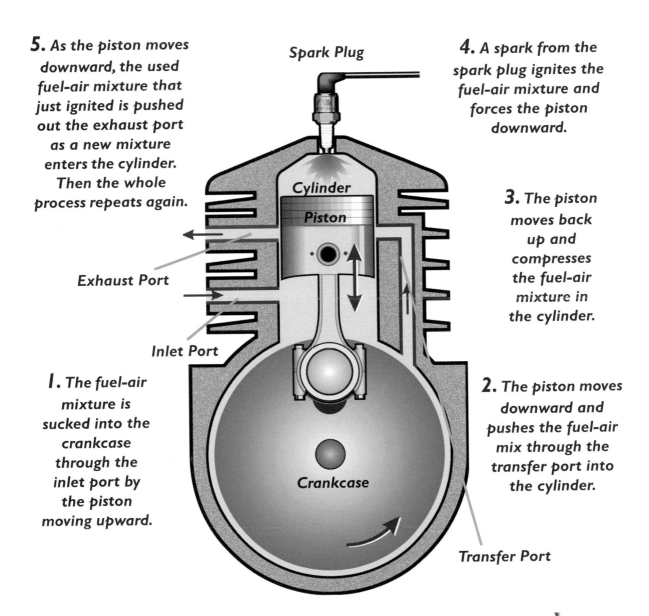

5. *As the piston moves downward, the used fuel-air mixture that just ignited is pushed out the exhaust port as a new mixture enters the cylinder. Then the whole process repeats again.*

Spark Plug

4. *A spark from the spark plug ignites the fuel-air mixture and forces the piston downward.*

Cylinder

Piston

3. *The piston moves back up and compresses the fuel-air mixture in the cylinder.*

Exhaust Port

Inlet Port

1. *The fuel-air mixture is sucked into the crankcase through the inlet port by the piston moving upward.*

Crankcase

2. *The piston moves downward and pushes the fuel-air mix through the transfer port into the cylinder.*

Transfer Port

Rules on Riding

Minibikes and minicycles usually aren't allowed on public streets. A street legal bike needs to have lights, mirrors, a horn, and a license. And, of course, the person driving the bike has to have a license. Because of these restrictions, you will probably need to either walk your minibike to the nearest trail, or have someone drive it to a trail for you.

Each state has different rules about where minibikes and minicycles can be driven. Unless you have a large piece of private property on which to drive, you will need to find out where the nearest trails are. Ask around. Find out from your local minibike or dirt bike shop.

A good place to find out where you can ride would be your state's Department of Natural Resources. Another place to try would be the Department of Parks and Tourism. Your state or national parks system might also be of help.

For beginning riders, a smooth course with small obstacles is the best place to start. A big back yard with only a few trees also works well. More advanced minibikers look for challenging trails. It is helpful to find out what kind of terrain you will be riding on before you get there. Always ride with at least one other person so that you can watch out for each other.

A smooth course with small obstacles is the best place to start getting to know your bike.

The Parts of a Mini

Starting a minibike involves either a pull-rope starter or a kick start. Just like a lawn mower, some minibikes have pull-rope starters. The bike that needs to be kick started is made with a crank that folds out along side the bike. The crank is made to be kicked with the rider's foot.

If your bike has an automatic clutch, make sure that the throttle is all the way off when you start it. If the throttle is stuck open at all, and you start the bike, the bike will take off without you. A good way to make sure this doesn't happen is to prop up the back wheel off the ground so it can turn freely. A stuck throttle is most likely to happen after the bike has been sitting for a while, as during the winter sitting in a cold garage.

Just as there are different ways of starting a minibike, there are also different kinds of brakes. Minibikes come with a foot brake, or a hand brake.

This minicycle uses a kick start that folds out from the side of the bike then folds back in after the bike is running. Notice the kick start crank is folded out.

Many of them have both. A hand brake can either be on the left side or on the right side of the handlebars.

The throttle is always on the right handlebar. When the rider twists the handle grip downwards, the throttle opens up. The farther the rider twists the throttle, the faster the bike goes.

The fenders on minibikes and minicycles sit high off the wheel to make room for the suspension. The forks need to be long so that the engine is held high off the ground, away from rocks and obstructions on the trails. The fenders will keep the majority of mud and rocks from flying up at the rider.

Many minibikes use an engine that is much like a lawn mower engine.

The forks also need to be long so when the bike hits the ground or runs into something on the trail, the springs and the forks will absorb the majority of the shock. A good suspension system will make a minicycle or minibike cost more money, but it's worth it if a rider is racing seriously or drives a lot on rough terrain. Heavy duty suspension is only needed for faster bikes. The shocks are often times adjustable. If the rider is heavy, the shocks should be tightened. If the rider is light, the shocks should be loosened.

Minibikes and minicycles usually don't have headlights or taillights. Some of the bigger-sized (100 cc or 125 cc) enduro minicycles use lights so that they can be street legal. Enduro minicycles are built to go long distances. People argue about whether or not these cycles should be considered motorcycles or minicycles. Either way, they are made to be street legal, so the law demands that they have lights and horns.

The tires on minibikes are small and wide. The tire's heavy tread works well in dirt, sand, mud, and gravel. A minicycle has slightly bigger tires, also with an aggressive tread. The tread helps the tire grip the ground better. A smooth tire would slip and slide through loose gravel, but a minibike's heavy treaded tire digs into the ground and pulls the bike along smoothly.

Minibikes have small, wide tires to help grip the ground.

How It Works

Learning about how a minibike works is very important. It helps the rider understand how to maintain a minibike. When the rider starts the engine, a mixture of gas and air is sucked into the cylinder. Then the piston inside the cylinder compresses the mixture in the small space at the top of the cylinder head. Next, a spark from the spark plug sets the fuel mixture on fire. The controlled explosion pushes the piston down, and the burned gas is sent out the exhaust pipe. Then the process starts all over again. This type of engine is called an internal combustion engine, because a small, measured explosion takes place inside the engine.

Before starting the engine, the rider needs to pull out or open the choke. This makes the air/gas mixture richer with gasoline.

**As with most minibikes and minicycles,
this minicycle uses a chain to drive the rear wheel.**

Pulling the starter rope or kicking down the crank turns over the pistons in the engine. This action starts the motor's cranks and pulleys. When the engine is first running, or idling, it's a good idea to give it a little more gas by turning the throttle, just to keep the engine going.

The power from the engine goes to the transmission. Most minibikes and minicycles use a chain to transfer the power from the transmission to the back wheel. The clutch is also an important part of the bike. Some bikes have automatic clutches, and the rider doesn't need to use a lever to manually pull in the clutch. If a bike has a manual clutch, the rider has to pull in the clutch lever and let off the throttle when he or she wants to change gears. The clutch engages and disengages the power from the motor to the transmission.

This minicycle uses a manual clutch, the lever is visible on the left handle grip. This cycle also uses five gears just like full-size motorcycles.

Taking Care of a Mini

Since there are a lot of parts on a minibike, there's a lot to maintain. Doing a few simple things will keep a minibike or minicycle running for a long time. Keeping the bike clean will make the bike last longer. You will be able to see if something is wrong with your bike if it is kept clean.

Another way to take care of your bike is to keep it lubricated. Keep the gas tank full. Check the oil level regularly. Keeping all parts oiled will make everything run smoothly.

It is a good idea to check the tires before a ride. Are the treads worn thin? Any bald spots or cracks? Check the tires for proper air pressure before you go for a ride. Also check the chain regularly. If it's too loose, it could jump off of the sprocket while you're driving down a trail. If a chain is too tight, it can wear down the teeth of the sprocket.

Make sure that all nuts and bolts are tight before riding. Bikes driven on trails are especially susceptible to bolts coming loose because of all the bangs and bumps a bike takes on a trail. Vibration from the engine also adds to the problem. Almost every part of the bike is in constant movement. As you get more experience with your bike, you will learn how to trouble shoot problems.

Each bike has different needs, so make sure you know what a bike requires before buying it. Asking a minibike or minicycle dealer about your model will give you helpful hints about how to make it last longer and run better. Keeping it clean will make it easier to resell, if you ever want to upgrade to a bigger bike.

Keeping your minibike or minicycle clean and in good working condition will make it safer to ride and easier to resell.

Mini Moves

Once you know the basics of driving a minibike or minicycle, learning a few more techniques will make trail riding easier. Tackling some basic maneuvers will get you through tight spots and will possibly save you from tumbling head over heels over your minibike. It is always important to choose your path carefully. Always scan ahead and look for obstacles. Choose the smoothest, most straight path on which to ride.

Riding up and down hills separates the beginner from the experienced rider. Going up a steep hill requires a lot of speed. Gain all the momentum you can at the bottom. Be careful not to gun it in the middle of the hill. This may cause your bike to flip over backwards. Expert riders lean forward and put their weight on the foot pegs while going up a hill.

Going downhill on a minibike, because of the small, stubby wheels, can flip the back wheel over the front wheel. To avoid this, smart riders choose their path at the top of the hill, and go slow enough to stay in control of the bike. Leaning back helps the rider to control the bike easier. At the bottom of the hill, choose a smooth path for an easy runoff.

The minibiker or minicycler will encounter many different kinds of terrain on the trail or dirt track. Soft sand presents obvious

problems. One way to get through sand is to gradually pick up speed, sit at the back of the seat for more rear wheel grip, and head in a straight path across the sand. Accelerating too much might cause the wheel to spin in the sand. If it's too hard to get through, jump off the bike and walk it through the sand with the motor running.

Mud is a different story. Most expert riders find knobby tires the best in mud. Going slowly with a small amount of acceleration—just enough to maintain speed—is the best thing to do. Keep a straight line because turning could cause the bike to slide and stop in the mud.

There are different riding techniques for different kinds of terrain.

Crossing water is easy as long as water doesn't get in the engine. Check the water depth before crossing, even if it just looks shallow. Experienced riders have found that crossing water should be done like crossing mud—slow and steady while going straight ahead. With a little practice most riders can master driving through rough terrain like mud, sand, and water.

Riding on a dirt track is also good practice. Racing minibikes and minicycles is a lot like the motocross races for full-sized motorcycles. The track is smaller and not as difficult, but just as fun! In racing, there are different classes, depending on the size of the engine and upon the age of the rider. Look for minibike or minicycle organizations in your state. Racing is a good way to meet other kids and to improve your riding skills.

Riding a minibike or minicycle is a lot of fun. These miniature cycles can take you on wild adventures to places you've never been before. Minis are a great place to start if you are serious about riding.

Kids as young as four can compete on minibikes and minicycles.

Glossary

Automatic Clutch - the engine automatically changes gears without the rider having to pull in a clutch lever and change gears manually.

Choke - adjusts the amount of gas and air mixture, and allows for a greater amount of gas in the engine to start the engine faster.

CC (Cubic Centimeters) - a way of measuring engine size.

Cylinder - the tube in an engine that houses the piston and fuel.

Forks - the tubes that connect the frame to the wheels.

Horsepower - a way of measuring engine size.

Industrial Engine - a gasoline powered engine used on lawn mowers or snowblowers, or anything else that needs a small engine.

Manual Clutch - the driver has to disengage the clutch while changing gears, instead of the engine doing it automatically.

Marketed - advertised with a certain group of people in mind.

Piston - the rod that pushes up and down inside the cylinder of an engine.

Private Property - restricted land that someone owns.

Street Legal - a vehicle that meets all the law requirements to be driven on streets and highways.

Suspension System - the system on a bike that makes the ride more cushioned and soft.

Telescopic Tubing - the tubing used on the forks of the bike.

Throttle - the grip on the handlebars that makes the bike accelerate.

Internet Sites

Minibike Central
http://www.geocities.com/MotorCity/7029/mini.html
This page shows pictures of awesome bikes and tells how to make them. It also has plenty of photos of minibikes and minicycles. This site will give you information on where to find minibikes and parts.

Pete's SOLO Disabled Motorcycle Project
http://www.btinternet.com/~chaloner/pete/pete.htm
This website is about a different kind of custom bike. The page is for disabled people who want to ride a motorcycle. See photos of this customized bike, and how it works.

The Dirt Bike Pages
http://www.off-road.com/orcmoto.html
This site has action photos of all kinds of dirt bikes, monthly columns and articles, and product reports. This site has important riding information, too.

Scooter Magazine Online
http://www2.scootermag.it/scooter/
This web site is fully devoted to motorscooters. Technique, developments, new models, tests, and track and road trials.

The Motorcycle Database
http://www.motorcycle.informaat.nl/ehome.html
Over 250 motorcycles, their specifications and pictures, and driver experiences from visitors. Pick the model and year of motorcycle you would like to see. Photos and detailed information is included. Lots to see!

Pass It On

Motorcycle Enthusiasts: educate readers around the country by passing on information you've learned about motorcycles. Share your little-known facts and interesting stories. Tell others what your favorite kind of motorcycle is or what your favorite type of riding is. We want to hear from you!

To get posted on the ABDO & Daughters website E-mail us at "Sports@abdopub.com"

Visit the ABDO Publishing Company website at www.abdopub.com

Index